D0848506

Row
the
Boat

A Never-Give-Up Approach to
Lead with Enthusiasm and Optimism
and Improve Your Team and Culture

JON
GORDON

P. J.
FLECK

WILEY

Published by John Wiley & Sons, Inc., Hoboken, New Jersey.
Published simultaneously in Canada.

Interior photography provided by the University of Minnesota, used with permission.

For general information on our other products and services or for technical support, please contact our Customer Care Department within the United States at (800) 762-2974, outside the United States at (317) 572-3993 or fax (317) 572-4002.

Wiley publishes in a variety of print and electronic formats and by print-on-demand. Some material included with standard print versions of this book may not be included in ebooks or in print-on-demand. If this book refers to media such as a CD or DVD that is not included in the version you purchased, you may download this material at http://booksupport.wiley.com. For more information about Wiley products, visit www.wiley.com.

Library of Congress Cataloging-in-Publication Data:
Names: Gordon, Jon, 1971- author. | Fleck, P. J., 1980- author.
Title: Row the boat : a never-give-up approach to lead with enthusiasm and optimism and improve your team and culture / Jon Gordon, P. J. Fleck.
Description: Hoboken, New Jersey : Wiley, [2021]
Identifiers: LCCN 2021010915 (print) | LCCN 2021010916 (ebook) | ISBN 9781119766292 (hardback) | ISBN 9781119766315 (adobe pdf) | ISBN 9781119766308 (epub)
Subjects: LCSH: Fleck, P. J., 1980- | Leadership. | Perseverance (Ethics) | Football—Coaching—Philosophy.
Classification: LCC HD57.7 .G666743 2021 (print) | LCC HD57.7 (ebook) | DDC 658.4/092—dc23
LC record available at https://lccn.loc.gov/2021010915
LC ebook record available at https://lccn.loc.gov/2021010916

Cover art: © SHUTTERSTOCK | KELVIN REYNOSO
Cover design: PAUL MCCRTHY

SKY10025784_042321

To my children, may you always see the good in everyone and dream BIG! Know that the dream is the journey.

To our players (current and former), may you never be a better football player than you are a person.

To our staff (current and former), thank you for always making our culture look so good.

To my wife, Heather, thank you for not allowing me to give up on R.T.B. Your strength, integrity, patience, and forgiveness inspire me daily.

To the children in the hospital, Row the Boat.

—P.J.

Contents

Introduction   *vii*

1 **The Man Behind the Boat** *(P.J. Fleck)*   **1**

2 **Questions** *(Jon Gordon)*   **17**

3 **The Origin of Row the Boat** *(P.J. Fleck)*   **21**

4 **The Philosophy of Row the Boat** *(P.J. Fleck)*   **27**

5 **Rowing the Boat at WMU** *(P.J. Fleck)*   **33**

6 **The Three Key Components of Row the Boat** *(P.J. Fleck)*   **51**

7 **A Bigger Opportunity and Challenge** *(Jon Gordon)*   **57**

8 **Rowing the Boat at the University of Minnesota** *(P.J. Fleck)*   **61**

9 **A Wave of Change** *(Jon Gordon)*   **81**

10 **Rowing through Adversity** *(P.J. Fleck)*   **85**

11 **Beyond Football** *(Jon Gordon)*   **93**

12 **The Impact of Row the Boat Beyond Football** *(P.J. Fleck)*   **97**

13   **Rowing into the Future** *(Jon Gordon)*   **103**

14   **Where Do You Row the Boat from
     Here?** *(P.J. Fleck)*   **107**

     Other Resources   *113*

     Other Books by Jon Gordon   *114*

Introduction

I've followed P.J. Fleck's coaching career for years, ever since he built the Western Michigan University (WMU) football team into a national powerhouse. I always admired his positive energy and passion and could tell he was a great culture builder and leader. I had also heard stories about him from Brad Black, whose company, HumanEx Ventures, performed the talent search and evaluation of head coaching candidates for WMU. Brad recommended to the leaders of WMU that they hire P.J. Fleck, despite his lack of qualifications, lack of head coaching experience, and unimpressive resume. Brad's assessment tools, used to evaluate people and predictive leadership performance, told him that P.J. would shine as a head coach and build a winning culture and team, and that's exactly what happened.

After proving himself as a successful head coach at Western Michigan, taking the program from 1–11 to 13–1 during his four years, P.J. Fleck was hired as the head coach of the University of Minnesota football team during a tumultuous time. Once again, P.J. turned around a program in need of a cultural change—academically, athletically, and socially—and built a winning culture both on and off the field. He created a team that won 11 games for the first time since 1904, achieved numerous academic records, and became a program that was more about serving and giving than just winning games.

After the season I invited P. J. to be on my podcast. One of my questions was about how he got into coaching. After the podcast I asked him to share more about his journey. The tale he told me was more than a story of his entry into coaching. It was about the man himself and what led him to become the kind of coach—and the kind of person—that he is.

—Jon Gordon

Proceeds from this book will help support the Fleck Family Fund at the University of Minnesota's Masonic Children's Hospital. For more information about Row the Boat and/or to support the foundation, please visit RowtheBoat.org.

Chapter 1

The Man
Behind the Boat

P.J. Fleck

2

Row the Boat

The Hard Way

Growing up as a runt on the block always seemed like an uphill challenge. Little did I know that the "underdog" way of life was paving the way for what I would need to succeed in a career that humbles and challenges the proudest and strongest of men. The chip on my shoulder started when I was young and eventually turned into a crack. I didn't feel I had to prove to anyone else that I could achieve my own dreams; rather, it was more that I had to prove to myself that I was everything I said I wanted to be.

I have always been referred to as the "King of the Toos." *Too* small, *too* short, *too* slow, *too* young, *too* inexperienced, and on and on—any kind of "too" you can think of, I've probably heard it. This kind of label makes people do two different things: run and forget, or play and prove. I chose to play and prove. My dad, Phil, always knew I was going to be an underdog with an undersized frame who would have to prove my worth on the sports field. My dad is 5-foot-5 and was a boxer in his youth. Whenever I would come home from shooting hoops or throwing the baseball or any other athletic endeavor, he would ask, "Are you done?" When I told him yes, he would reply, "Well, that's fine, but don't forget, there is always someone out there taking one more rep than you just did." Early on he was instilling in me that my path would *not* be easy and I would have to work to achieve success. He knew I had very big dreams, and he prepared my mind to think, focus, and respond the right way.

How did he do this? Well, when I was growing up you didn't have to show your birth certificate, fingerprints, and

3

bloodwork just to prove your age. (I'm joking, but you get the idea.) If there was an 8-year-old baseball team, everyone just assumed all members of the team were 8. They took your word for it. My dad made sure that I was always "playing up," so when I was 8, I played on the 10-year-old team. When I was 10, I played on the 11- or 12-year-old team. I learned at an early age that there would always be people out there with an easier path than me. I saw how they were more skilled, more physically mature, bigger, stronger, and faster. However, the skill they possessed was only part of the equation. Being younger and a late bloomer, I was going to have to find other ways to succeed and win. I started to value the "talent" of a person at an early age more than just the "skill."

Knowing that I wasn't the most skilled on the field and being smaller, shorter, and slower than most of the other kids on my team and in the league, I recognized that talent was much more than physical ability and stature. I discovered that *talent* (the how, heart, spirit, creativity, unconquerable will, effort, soul, passion, ability to be a great teammate, and refuse-to-lose mentality) were a big part of success and who I was, and I could use *my* talent to my advantage. I had to play smarter, work harder, and find ways to do it better for longer. My game had to be different. I didn't have a choice if I wanted to succeed. People often say that talent is something you are born with and skill is something you develop. However, I believe "skill" is what you were born with based on genes from your parents and "talent" is the unmeasurable force that allows your skill to develop into something really special based on all the experiences in your life.

Not only did my dad teach that the talent of a person mattered the most, but he also made me see that I could connect my teammates and friends and other boys who lived on my block. Even though I was the youngest on the block, I wasn't afraid to talk to anyone. I was very confident and kind as a young person and saw the good in everyone. I was always taught that there is so much more good in a person than there is bad, so find the good, bring it out, give others the benefit of the doubt. Judge those on how they treat you and stand up for others who don't stand up for themselves.

But the road to prove myself was longer than most because I was the youngest and got picked on more than the other kids. For instance, one afternoon after walking up the hill from trading baseball cards with the kids on the block, some of the older kids tore up my cards and sent me home with my tail between my legs for not trading my best cards with them. I arrived home sad, mad, and frustrated. My dad took one look at me and said, "You have two options— sit here and cry, or go make it work." Simple yet powerful. It was my job to find a way to make the situation work after being embarrassed and humiliated by the kids on the block. "Find a way" was the lesson: even on the days when you don't feel like it, go make it work with the other kids on the block who just humiliated you in front of the others. Sit here and cry or go find a way to make it work for you.

One Christmas I received a pair of boxing gloves and we used them to box each other in the street. The older kids would assign who was going to fight, and then each fighter got one glove since mine were the only pair. Even though I was the youngest, everyone loved to watch me fight because I wouldn't quit. The older kids would give me the left-handed glove, knowing I'm right-handed, and give the right-handed glove to the older kid I had to box. Then the older kids would come to *my* corner to help me in between rounds and cheer me on. I used to think they just loved seeing me get the crap kicked out of me, but as I matured, I understood what they liked most was that I never quit. Did I get the crap kicked out of me? Yes, most of the time, but I never stopped fighting and that's what they loved to see. This would help me develop leather skin. I called it developing leather skin for all the tough situations in my life ahead that I would have to face later on.

Kaneland High School in Illinois is where I truly started to find my passions on the field and courts. I ended up being a three-time, three sport All-State athlete in football, basketball, and track. I averaged 24.8 points per game in basketball (most of my points came off of hustle on the defensive side of the court). On the track I ran the 300 intermediate hurdles and the 400 (two gut races that were close to each other in the meets) along with triple jump, long jump, 4×1, 4×4, and high hurdles. In football I was a wide receiver on a back-to-back 14–0 Illinois State Championship team and set numerous state and school records in receiving. However, at the end of my high school career I was 5-foot-9 and 150 pounds soaking wet, and ran a 4.8 40. So, as you can imagine the scholarships were not flying in. Then came a summer football camp at Northern Illinois University. This would be the first event that would make my football career what it is today.

Northern Illinois University was located 20 miles west of Sugar Grove, where I basically grew up. I went to the summer camp before my senior year in high school. I didn't have the typical size, speed, and frame to pass the eye test for a division one scholarship. So I had to go to a summer camp to get looks from college coaches. It was one of those intense camps where you practiced and played hard for four days, three practices a day, in helmets and shoulder pads, on the old Astroturf. I knew the only way I was going to be noticed and respected was if everyone could see my heart and consistency of effort, and truly trust that I was the real deal. I left that camp with turf burns all over my body. I dove for every ball, caught every ball thrown to me, and left no doubt in the coach's mind that I could play at the D1 level despite my size! It paid off. During the last week of official visits at NIU I was offered the last available full-ride scholarship that year by Head Coach Joe Novak to play football and get my elementary education degree. All the coaches who worked for him at the time told him I was too small, too slow, and there was no way I was good enough. He told them all this was "his" last scholarship and he was taking me no matter what. This one decision by my former head coach, taking a chance on me, would change my life's path forever.

During my time at NIU I saw us go from a team that had gone 3–30 over a 3-year span before our class would enroll to a 10–2 season my senior year, beating Alabama in Tuscaloosa, Maryland at home, and Iowa State at home, all in the same year. The turnaround at NIU was complete and we laid the foundation for the future success of the program. I finished my career by setting numerous school records as an All-MAC wide receiver, an academic All-American, and

7

earned a bachelor's degree in elementary education. My individual and our team accomplishments weren't easy. We had a saying back then that still resonates with the NIU program today: "The hard way!" Our path was hard, but I've learned the hard way is usually the right way.

Make the Most of Your Opportunities

Not many people thought I would ever play in the NFL. Why should they? I didn't have the prototypical size or speed of an NFL wide receiver. However, in 2004 I was picked up as an undrafted free agent with the San Francisco 49ers. We had 14 WRs on the depth chart the day I arrived at mini-camp. Teams usually keep five or six receivers on their team. Based on the receivers already on the team and the new draft picks, about eight people were competing for one spot on the active roster and one practice squad spot. The first mini-camp was a three-day camp. I understand now, since coaching in the NFL, that the very first mini-camp says a lot about how the coaches feel about you and how many reps you may get. As an undrafted rookie I didn't receive any significant reps all weekend at that first mini-camp.

During our last day, I wondered if my chance would ever come or if I would be cut before getting to show them what I was made of. Fast-forward to the end of the last day. Coach Dennis Erickson gathered the team at the end of practice and told us we were going to have a conditioning test. My ears perked up like a dog does when you ask them if they want to go outside and play. This was my chance, no matter what Coach Erickson made us do, I *had* to find a way not only to do well, but to win the contest. This was the only way I was going to get noticed by the staff, players, and management. It was the *only* way I would be able to see another day in a 49ers uniform. It was the only way at this point I could show them my talent and heart! This was it.

When Coach told us we were going to do the beep test (The Pacer), I thought to myself, "I have actually done this test before." It consists of a series of beeps that steadily get faster as the test goes on. A beep starts you and a beep ends you. You must beat the beep to advance on to the next round. I still remember to this day the sound of the beep, the focus I had to beat the beep, and who was running with me. Jeff Garcia, the former San Francisco quarterback, had set a franchise record in this test with somewhere around 140 beeps. I didn't know that going into the test; all I knew was that if I wanted to see tomorrow and not get cut, I was going to have to win the whole thing.

As the race went on it came down to two people: Brandon Doman, the rookie QB from BYU, and me. We were stride for stride through 70/80/90/100 beeps. The team had surrounded us both, as if they were watching an impromptu race on the school playground. At 110/120, still neck-and-neck, wobbling just to stand up. Then 130/135. On rep 140 we both crossed the finish line and collapsed. It was over. We *both* won and finished at the exact same time and same place.

Immediately we were celebrated by teammates and coaches. Everyone knew Brandon, but through the course of the race I made them know me. In that 20-minute race, my heart, passion, and character were on full display, witnessed by anyone who was watching. I gave them all a reason to not cut me just yet! Before we left the field, Coach Erickson said,

"Brandon, you and number 10, that freaking warrior, break it down." So we did, together! I'm not sure everyone knew my name at this point, but at least number 10 had made it to tomorrow. Going from getting cut to lasting two and a half years in the league started by just gutting through a playground race that changed the course of my future forever. We never know when that unexpected challenge might be what sets our future course.

Hard Work, Opportunity, and Fate

In 2004 I made the practice squad and played against New England in the last game of the year, for my first true Sunday NFL game! Dream complete! The next week Dennis Erickson was fired and was replaced by Mike Nolan, a man who would shape my coaching and playing career forever. I wear a tie on the sideline for two men who made me who I am as a coach: Mike Nolan and Jim Tressel. If it wasn't for them, I wouldn't be a coach today.

In 2005, I made it all the way up to the number 3 WR on the depth chart. I was the starting slot WR, but in the pre-season against Oakland I blew out my shoulder covering a kickoff. I was put on injured reserve that next week and my season was over. Mike Nolan called me up to his office and gave me the option of going home to get my surgery and rehab (which most players do when their season is over) or staying and helping coach our young WRs. Jerry Sullivan was our WR coach at the time, and he allowed me to work with the young players before our morning meetings. I was going to help the same guys that I would be competing against next year for playing time. But I wanted to help the team, and the team came first. So each day I met with the rookies in the morning to help them install our offense for the week and after practice I would work with them on the field. Coach Nolan's office overlooked the practice facility, so he saw me work daily with the young players.

The next summer in the off-season leading up to training camp, I blew out my hamstring. Again, another setback put me two weeks behind everyone and would make me miss time in training camp as well. Coach Nolan called me into his office one morning and gave me the news no player wants to receive. It was an unusual setting because his wife was in his office as well. I thought to myself, "He's going to cut me with his wife listening? What a jerk!" Kathy was giddy too, like she was excited I was getting cut. Salt in the wound. Yes, he did cut me. That was the point of me going up there. However, what came next truly shocked me. After he cut me, in the next sentence he offered me a coaching job on his staff. That's why Kathy was smiling. She knew I was going to be offered a job.

"What kind of job?" I asked.

Coach Nolan replied, "I don't know yet. I don't have a job open but I'm going to invent one for you because I think you should get into coaching."

I was taken aback. I was devastated that I had just gotten cut, but then I was immediately offered a job. Talk about experiencing a wide range of emotions in one moment. An NFL head coach had been watching me coach the young players, and he believed I could be an asset to his organization! As with most things in my life, I could only get somewhere I dreamed of if someone gave me a shot and believed in me enough to get there. Mike Nolan did. I was honored. As it turned out, though, I didn't take the job, because another life-altering call was one day away.

After a lot of prayer and signs of faith, I came to the conclusion that my football playing career was over. An NFL head coach thought enough of me to ask me to start my coaching career. I always wanted to teach. This would be the best of both worlds, teaching and coaching football! After some long thought and not passing a physical with the Chicago Bears, I decided I was going to take Coach Nolan up on his offer.

Just as I was about to call him, my phone rang with a call from Columbus, Ohio. I picked it up to find Jim Tressel on the line. I had never met him, but Jim asked if I was interested in becoming the offensive and special teams' graduate assistant (GA) at Ohio State! I thought to myself, "I've never met him, I never applied, I'm about to take the job in SF, how in the world does he know me and why does he want me?" It turned out that Mike Sabock, who coached me at NIU, was a fraternity brother of Jim's and knew I wanted to coach, let Jim know I got cut in training camp and was now moving into coaching, and that if any jobs opened up, I'd be perfect.

As fate would have it, Coach Tres actually had a spot open because the offensive GA who was supposed to have the job couldn't get into grad school at the last minute, so they were scrambling to find someone to take the job late in the process. And that's how I got my coaching start—fate and people believing in me and giving me an opportunity to prove myself.

I told Coach Nolan I was taking the OSU job and explained that I needed a clean cut from the NFL at the time because if I coached the same guys whom I thought I was better than, it would be hard for me to move on from playing to start my new career. He understood and to this day is one of my biggest mentors in my career and in my life. As I said, I wear a tie on the sideline for the two men who wore ties when they were head coaches so people know it's because of them that I am coaching on that sideline. I honor them every game and will always do so. I wouldn't be where I am without Jim Tressel and Mike Nolan. My gratitude runs deep, and I will always represent those men in the best way I can.

I was a coach and I now had the opportunity to pass on what I learned from the coaches who invested in me. My coaches were and still are the greatest influences in my life. From my time at Kaneland High School under Hall of Fame Coach Joe Thorgesen, where I learned that a group of individuals is not a team, but if those individuals can bond together around common goals, drown out the outside critics, and truly put aside personal success for the team, they can accomplish far more than a simple group of individuals. From Coach Erickson I learned to believe in someone's talent, not just their skill. Skill can only take us so far; the ultimate competitor is someone whose talent matches their skill. Coach Nolan taught me about class and is still the classiest man I have ever met. Everything he does, he does the right way and with class, even the hard conversations and the hard days.

Coach Tressel taught me to care for *everyone* inside the organization. Everyone's job matters and if you care more about them as people rather than as players or employees, you'll get their best. Coach T always taught me that we don't have jobs without players, so everything inside your program should be about them. Each day find creative ways to make the student athletes better students, players, fathers, husbands, and men. Coach Novak at NIU taught me to take a chance on someone whom others might be overlooking. Everyone needs a shot, a break, and someone else to believe in them to get them going as he did for me. Coach Greg Schiano at Rutgers taught me how to demand the most out of myself and be the most detailed and incredibly organized coach I could be. He also taught me always to coach your coaches to become better men and teachers. Finally, I have learned from every assistant coach with whom I worked with. A good coach learns not only from the other coaches around them, but from their players too. Learning and growth are keys to success.

Chapter 2

Questions

Jon Gordon

18

Row the Boat

P.J.'s back story is very powerful. I didn't know how he got his start or all he had to endure to become a coach. I didn't know about the underdog he was or how hard he worked to prove himself. I just knew he was the "Row the Boat" guy. I was now even more intrigued and wanted to know where Row the Boat came from. His answers were so compelling that I knew they needed to be shared with everyone who wanted to build a great team. P.J. and I decided to write this book both to encourage you and to help you and your team grow stronger together with the Row the Boat principles.

The chapters that follow are based on a series of questions I've asked P.J. His answers will bring the Row the Boat principles and movement to life. You will learn how a leader with a powerful framework who is driven by a core set of principles and values can transform a culture and a team. You will understand that when a team buys into the culture and believes in an idea that becomes the heart and soul of team, amazing things are possible. You will realize that Row the Boat is not some simple cliché or catchphrase or theme. It is the essence of what P.J. and his teams believe, value, and live.

In this spirit, the first subject I asked P.J. about was where he came up with Row the Boat. His answer inspired me and brought me to tears at the same time.

Chapter 3

The Origin of
Row the Boat

P.J. Fleck

22

Row the Boat

Pain and Purpose

February 9, 2011, was the day I lost my son, Colton, right after his birth due to complications with his heart and lungs. I was coaching at Rutgers under Greg Schiano at the time and was thankful that he allowed me to go back and forth to Children's Hospital of Philadelphia (CHOP) multiple times for testing on Colton prior to him being born. At one visit I received unexpected and devastating news. I was told that Colton would not live long after his birth and there wasn't much anyone could do about it. The news knocked the wind out of me. I literally couldn't breathe. I felt like I was suffocating from the heaviness of what I had just heard.

How could this be? How could he *not* make it? How come a doctor couldn't fix it? Where was God? I was filled with questions, confusion, and anger. I felt numb to life after the reality of the situation hit me that my son was going to die soon after being born. Then, when he was born, everything seemed fine. "Look . . . he's breathing," I said with excitement and hope. "Is there anything we can do *now* to save him?" There was nothing they could do. After a few minutes on Earth, Colton James Fleck had passed away.

Those were some of the slowest, most numbing, and *realest* few minutes of my life. Holding your son as he takes his last breath changes you for the rest of your life, whether you're ready for it or not. I felt like my life was over. I didn't feel strong enough to overcome this tragedy. I wanted to give up, to quit and never revisit that time in my life. The grief stages had taken over my every move, mentally, physically, and emotionally. My thoughts were consumed by a cloud of darkness

23

The Origin of Row the Boat

that seemed only to get darker with every passing day. It felt like the pain would never go away and time moved so slowly. Most of us have been in a very low place at some point in our lives. It's okay to grieve, cry, and feel pain. After all, we are human beings with real feelings and emotions. I was there after Colton passed away, but thankfully there came a moment when my pain became the major part of my purpose.

Row the Boat

I decided I was not going to let his name or legacy ever fade away. I was never going to forget about him and act like it didn't happen. I wanted to come up with something that would keep Colton's name and memory alive forever. I wanted to move forward in a positive direction and use what happened to me to connect others in the future who might experience something similar. I wanted a powerful analogy and symbol that would demonstrate the core of who I was and the difference I wanted to make and honor Colton in the process.

I wanted to give my children something to live by, a lifestyle, a way of handling adversity, tragedy, triumph, failing, conquering, and doubting. I wanted to create something that gave back to the community I was coaching in, a charity of some sort that the community could rally behind. Finally, I wanted to make sure that when I did become a head coach, I could share my story with the team, staff, university, and community to connect people from all walks of life with a powerful message *never to give up!* So I had to come up with what I wanted the concept to be, how it would look, and how it would impact others during my life and career.

I didn't know when I would become a head coach, but I knew I wanted to make a great impact on others when I did.

At Rutgers, Greg Schiano had a slogan, "Keep chopping," from his cultural saying, "The Chop." Take the axe and just keep hitting the mark over and over and over, and eventually the tree will fall. I really loved this concept, and still do to this day. I believe in fate and that everything happens for a reason, so when Colton took his last breath at CHOP, I asked myself, "Is this a coincidence? I think not." I was inspired and compelled to create an overarching message that would guide my personal and professional life and the teams I would lead in the future.

I've always loved boats and water. They make me feel at peace. There is something about the tranquility of water that brings me to a special place mentally and emotionally. Being a teacher at heart, I love sharing simple, powerful lessons and always look for the simplest way to teach a life lesson to connect with my players. This led me to one of the most memorable nursery rhymes of all time, "Row, Row, Row Your Boat." I realized it was time to *row the boat*!

An Opportunity to Row the Boat

Fast-forward to 2013. I was fortunate enough that an athletic director from Western Michigan University named Kathy Beauregard took a chance on me, believed in me, and made me the new head coach. At the time, I had just turned 32 and was coaching wide receivers for the Tampa Bay Buccaneers in the NFL under Greg Schiano. I loved being back in the NFL but I couldn't resist the opportunity to lead my own program and team. I became the youngest head coach in the country in the same conference I played in. It was a perfect fit. WMU hadn't won a championship since 1988 and the only one before that was in 1966. It also had never been to a New Year's Six bowl, never beat a ranked team, never won a bowl game, and so on. It might not have seemed like a good job, but I felt it was perfect for me and a great opportunity to establish a brand-new culture to connect the past to the present.

So I took the job, and in the introductory press conference, I introduced Row the Boat for the first time. Not many people in my life even knew I had been coming up with this for two years and was ready to share it. Some told me I was crazy to blend my personal life with the football life. Back then, authenticity and vulnerability weren't seen as desirable characteristics in coaches. Row the Boat also had absolutely nothing to do with a Bronco (the WMU mascot) or Kalamazoo, so to many it didn't make any sense and didn't seem like a good fit. I learned that if you are going to brand and make public something so personal, you had better be confident enough and ready for the critics to attack it and not take it personally.

Truthfully, it's easier said than done. But I knew it was right for me and for this program and so I pressed on. Did it work? Not at first. But before I share that story, I want to share the Row the Boat Philosophy with you.

Chapter 4

The Philosophy of Row the Boat

P.J. Fleck

Row the Boat

"Row the Boat" is a never-give-up mantra and an approach to life and work that anyone can adopt and implement. It's a standard that says your life will not be defined by circumstances or events. When adversity hits, and I guarantee it will, you will not allow a situation or a person to discourage you or affect your way of life. Rather, with enthusiasm, inspiration, and optimism, you will create your way of life. Row the Boat is about being proactive, not reactive or perfect. Regardless of what happens, you have already decided that you are going to keep moving forward in a positive way.

This perspective separates the elite from the average in sports and in life. The way you handle one thing is the way you handle everything, and you must handle it at an elite level. If you want to be elite, you have to stay in the now and keep moving forward. The *now* matters. You can't let your situations define you. With attitude and effort, you must define your situation.

Row the Boat is also a leadership approach that inspires and empowers the people in your boat to row with the same power, tempo, direction, and speed toward the vision you have for your team and organization. In tough times, *row*. In successful times, *row*. In times of uncertainty, *row*. In times of struggle, *row*. When the waves of life are stormy and dangerous and they rock your boat to the core, *row*. On days when the seas are calm and glisten with sunshine, *row*. In the end, why we row, how we row, and the way we row through all of it will dictate our path and determine how far we go.

Future

Rowing is very different from paddling. When rowing a boat, your back is to the bow (the front of the boat), which

29

represents the future. This means that as you are rowing, you can't see what's ahead of you in that very moment. None of us have any idea what the future holds for us. We don't know what tomorrow or even the next moment brings. Life can change in a moment. The uncertainty is what defines life!

Present

When *you* row the boat, you row in the present moment with your own oar, which is the *only* thing you can control right now! Making choices and decisions of how you handle and think about the *now* is a choice of one person: you. You are either rowing or you are not. You either quit in the now or you don't. There is no in between. Don't let the fear of the future or the pain from the past stop you from rowing toward your dreams.

Past

When rowing, you are facing the stern (the back of the boat), which symbolizes the past. Your eyes see where you have already been. With every stroke, you see the horizon and what just happened. The only thing we should do with the past is learn from it. With every stroke, we grow. It's not easy to let the past go, but doing so allows us to focus our energy on the present. After all, the next stroke is what needs our energy and attention.

This approach is life-changing. Learn from and embrace your past to create your future. Row in the present and be optimistic and hopeful. Know that the next stroke of the oar is what's needed to overcome and conquer your challenges and create your future. Don't let the sea dictate where you go. You decide, and you keep rowing. Learn from your past, row in the present, and prepare for whatever comes your way.

The most important thing is to keep on rowing.

Chapter 5

Rowing the Boat at WMU

P. J. Fleck

34

Row the Boat

A Difficult Task

Who would have thought that Row the Boat would be thrust into motion two short years after Colton had passed? In 2011, I had started to formulate the process of building a culture that would be positive, energetic, philanthropic, and proactive. In 2013, I began to create this culture when Kathy Beauregard, the athletic director at WMU, not only gave me the opportunity to be a 32-year-old head coach, but also allowed me to be *me* and turn around a program that had never won a bowl game, never beat a Top 25 team, never been ranked in the AP poll, never won 10 games or more in a season, never had a Heisman candidate, and never hosted ESPN's College GameDay.

Many people advised me to wait and take a "better" job. But I've never known what the phrase "better job" means. Every job has its own challenges. As Jim Tressel used to say, "jobs are open for a reason." As I talked with many of my mentors about taking the job, the same things came up. One, this is a really tough job. Two, you're so young at 32 and if it doesn't work, you might have taken your shot on the wrong job and now you are 35, fired, and will never be a head coach again. And many advised me to stay in the NFL and get a "better job" in college or the NFL down the road.

One particular conversation with one of my mentors really opened my eyes to exactly what I was being offered. That person said to me, "Who the hell do you think you are? Head coaching jobs don't come around very often. There are only around 125 college Division 1, FBS jobs in America. How could one of those *not* be good enough for a 32-year-old

35

coming up in this profession?" After that discussion, I knew that what I was being offered was a goldmine. It was going to be challenging and would test me every day, but I was determined to make WMU *the* job and make WMU *the* place for moments and memories, and to make the "nevers" a thing of the past. I was taught a long time ago, "Nevers aren't forever!"

People often ask me the hardest part about taking over a football program. Without a doubt it's the process of changing the culture. I define change as truthful listening and define culture as connecting people positively. Therefore, it's changing people's thoughts, perspectives, and beliefs from "We haven't" and "We can't" to "We will" and "We can." The Row the Boat philosophy is a crucial part of facilitating this change because our beliefs, focus, and effort are controllable. We don't have to let our energy wane and then give up. We can always sacrifice and do more for others and ourselves. We can all learn from our past and move forward to create our future.

A big reason why WMU was so attractive to me was based on what they hadn't accomplished. We could get people to accomplish their dreams, do what they once thought they couldn't, and leave a legacy. We could truly put our stamp on the program, university, and community. We weren't going to simply *try* to get this done. We were going to actually *do* it. Failure was not an option. Turning the boat around was not an option.

Failing, however, was necessary and failing was going to happen, a lot. We define failing as growth and failure as quitting. We were all taking a risk but risk is not inherently bad. Risk just tests how much you need something to work and whether you can live with the result, no matter what that result ends up being. You can't leave a mark or create a legacy if the road is an easy one. Teddy Roosevelt said, "Never throughout history has a man who lived a life of ease left a name worth remembering." WMU was definitely not going to be easy, but it was absolutely worth it to me to give everything I had to make it work. This job had opportunity written all over it. I knew that by blending the Row the Boat culture with WMU's past tradition, stirred with the elite city of Kalamazoo and mixing with elite people, we could accomplish whatever we dreamed of. It was time to stop talking and start rowing, because we had a lot of work to do.

The Big Dig

I compare building a program to building a house. In year one, you have to dig down deep on the plot of land you have been granted. At WMU I introduced Row the Boat the entire first off-season. I shared how we were going to row together no matter what happened and create a lifestyle that would pave the way for the rest of our player's lives on and off the field. The first year of changing the culture is so hard because it's new for everyone. It's the first time for everything. From winter conditioning, spring ball, training camp, and everything else on the field, to cultural beliefs, rules, and different situations—everything is being learned and everything is new. I have learned a saying in the course of my career:

Bad teams, nobody leads.

Average teams, coaches lead.

Elite teams, players lead.

The more urgently your team can learn the culture, the faster you can get to a player-led team and accelerate winning.

It's more difficult to win when everyone is still learning the culture for the first time. In 2013 at WMU, we were a long way from the mastery stage where our players and coaches could teach our culture to others and lead everyone inside the organization. However, every coaching change has to start somewhere, and we were off and running, doing our best to create positive change as fast as possible. Mike Tyson once said, "Everyone has a plan until they get punched in the mouth." That might be the best way to describe our first year at WMU. We finished our first season 1–11. I saw some publications that ranked head coaches that season. I was dead last! Now you're probably thinking, "Why am I reading a book about the culture of someone who won one game?" If that was the end of the story I wouldn't disagree with you. However, it was that result and this first year that made our program so special. Year one, the dig, we found out a lot about life and ourselves that would pave the way for future success.

I believe in learning from my past in order to create a better future. I'm always thinking of what I can learn from it and what I need to do to improve. Our second game was the hardest lesson I have had to live through when it comes to coaching football. We had just come off a hard-fought game at Michigan State where we actually played well and kept the game close all the way to the end. We ended up losing; however, I thought we might have a good football team if we competed like that each week. We weren't the most skilled team, but our players played hard in that first game.

Then came our home opener at Waldo Stadium the next week against Nicholls State. They had just lost to Oregon by 63 in their first game. All week long I kept hearing from boosters, donors, friends, administration, and family, "Well, it was hard to lose week 1, but your student-athletes played so hard. At least this week you'll get your first win as a head coach and we can get that off your plate." Easy as that, huh? Just show up as 29.5-point favorites and get our first win in front of a huge home crowd at Waldo stadium in the WMU Row the Boat (RTB) era and move on to bigger things. Well, that's why you play the game. Nicholls State beat us 27–23 in the first home game of my career, in front of about 25,000 fans as 29.5-point underdogs. As you can imagine, RTB took a little hit to its credibility that day.

It didn't get much better as the season went along. We won only one game against UMASS 31–30 on the last play of the game. I learned really fast that you better be authentic and truly believe in your culture because it will be harshly criticized when expectations don't meet reality. *Nobody* in Kalamazoo wanted to Row the Boat anymore. RTB became a joke, and a punchline. To add more insult to injury, I was going through a divorce during that season. The jokes and jabs got worse by the day. My own doubts, fears, and insecurities welled up inside me. The media was constantly asking me, "Well, RTB didn't work, so what's the next slogan?" I was already getting questions about my job security. You can imagine what my coaches and players must have been thinking and feeling.

Little did people know, *this* was the time we were rowing the most. RTB was not created for easy, calm seas and

39

Rowing the Boat at WMU

comfort. It was made to help people get through the most difficult times of their lives. Row the Boat came into existence just in time and at the right time!

I struggled with the mocking of RTB because of where it originated in my life and Colton's passing. However, I knew most people didn't know the back story. They didn't know how personal it was and I had to be okay with people attacking RTB once I put it out in public. The risk of changing lives forever was worth it for me. To do good with it and help inspire people significantly in so many ways was my focus. Nothing was going to get me off my *row*. The noise of the naysayers was something I had to tune out and also understand it would only get louder. However, the type of people we had in the program was about to show in a powerful way.

When you're learning from your players as much as they are learning from you, you know you have a genuine culture. Zach Terrell, future Campbell Trophy winner and our QB at the time who is arguably one of the greatest players in MAC history, got up in front of the team in a team meeting, stopped me mid-sentence, and asked the team to pray for me and for the challenges I was leading them through, for the personal life challenges I was going through, and for the courage to not give up on Row the Boat. Wow! It was so powerful coming from one of our players. I knew we were on our way to having that genuine culture.

After that moment I never questioned my players' buy-in or commitment to our program and each other. I knew we could get out of the storms we were rowing in because we had people with compassion, love, persistence, and the ability to keep on rowing. They cared for others as much as they cared about themselves. We had to recruit more people like Zach who wanted to live their best life academically, athletically, socially, and spiritually, and that's exactly what we did. We were going to embrace our past to create our future. Everything we were going through as coaches and players was integral to set up our success down the road. In 2013, the ones who believed stayed, and the ones who didn't believe left. Sometimes addition by subtraction is necessary. By the end of that year, the dig was complete and we were ready to move on to the next phase of building our culture.

Pouring the Foundation

I call year two of building a culture *pouring the foundation*. After the hole has been dug, the concrete is poured in and left to harden. This is when you truly set the foundation of the culture. 2014 started out a lot like year one in many ways in terms of outcomes. I was personally struggling with not seeing the results, not having proof that my plan worked, and people doubting our program everywhere. I even started to doubt whether I should even be using this Row the Boat mantra anymore. Then, as with most life-changing moments, we meet someone who brings us back to life, gives us direction, and becomes the most influential person we have ever met. My wife, Heather, was that person for me. I have been taught people come into our lives for a reason, a season, and/or a lifetime. I could see early on that Heather was going to be all three. I met Heather at one of the lowest points in my life: after a 1–11 season, recently divorced, far from God, and doubting everything I once believed in. At one point I

41

thought of not using RTB anymore because I didn't know if I could handle the criticism it was taking and the lack of proof it worked. I was at my worst and had to lead a football team that needed to see my best.

Heather changed everything. She would not allow me to give up on RTB. She made me realize that the platform I had been given by God was meant to be used to bring more good to the world than just winning football games. She taught me that the hard part about being the standard is you are the standard, not just sometimes but all the time! The way you live your life is much bigger than what your title is. On one of our first dates, I asked her, "You do know who I am, right? I'm the 1–11, divorced football coach everyone is talking about in town." She looked at me intensely and replied, "Well . . . looks like I'm the girl who's going to change your life." I think she stole that line from the movie *Friends with Benefits* with Justin Timberlake and Mila Kunis, but she has been that girl from the day I met her. Heather has never allowed me *not* to be who I say I am, which is all about accountability.

I changed so much after meeting Heather. She's Italian mixed with a little Irish, so you can just feel the feistiness, selflessness, loyalty, love, heart, beauty, and drive. Her spirit and passion for RTB wouldn't allow me to quit on Colton, my other kids, our players, our community, our fans (even though we didn't have many at that time), and most importantly she wouldn't let me quit on myself. She saw the best in me, saw my purpose and was going to make sure RTB would be at the forefront of year two and the rest of our lives together. She has sacrificed so much of her own life for our football life and has helped make a huge difference in the lives of others in the communities which we have lived. If it wasn't for Heather, I'm not sure RTB would even be here and I'm not sure if I would even be in coaching.

Okay, let's get back to football and year two. We started the season 2–3 and weren't looking like a very connected team just yet. We were a better team (after all, 2–3 is better than 1–11), but not an elite team yet. We had just signed one of the greatest recruiting class in the history of the MAC and WMU. We knew that the guys who embraced RTB during 1–11 would be the same people who would invest the most to make sure we turned the program around. The old saying "The more you give up, the harder it is to quit" came into play with this team. A lot of these young men gave up the opportunity to play for "bigger" programs to join the RTB culture at WMU and accomplish things that had never been done before.

We started 16 freshmen and decided to invest in the youth of the program. We knew it could get worse before it got better, but the investment was worth it to us. Give me elite people and I'll teach them the rest. People win! We knew they were going to take their lumps early on, but also knew they were the right young men who would transform early failing into future growth and become stronger through the process. These were young men of character who would embrace adversity, not run from it.

The turning point for the RTB culture came while playing Ball State in Muncie on October 11, 2014. We were down at halftime 31–14, getting ready to go to 2–4 on the year. The week prior against Toledo, we lost in overtime when we missed an extra point that bounced off the upright.

Emotionally, I knew that this game could have the potential to either propel us or decimate us. Timing is everything and I knew at halftime I had to come up with something—a big moment, a speech they would truly remember. I gave it some thought, walked into the locker room, and proclaimed, *"When you are tired of being average, you're not!"* Then I walked out.

It wasn't what I planned; it was just what I felt at that time. It was all I could say. It was one of those moments when you have a plan, but the minute you feel the pulse of the room, you don't use that plan. Well, we came out of halftime and outscored Ball State 28–7 in the second half to win the game 42–38. If you watch the replay from the sideline it looks like we won the Super Bowl on the last play. For us it felt that way. We knew this win would capture the trust and belief in the RTB culture, and it did. We went on to win five

more games in a row, went 8–4 on the year, and played in the Famous Idaho Potato Bowl. We finished 8–5. Our coaching staff was named Coach of the Year and the foundation was set. We now had an elite platform to build our "house." Our team was tired of being average. They were learning that their culture of togetherness made them *elite*.

Creating Our Framework

The third year of building our culture was focused on creating our framework. People were going to be able to "drive by" our lot and see a house truly going up. We used words like connectivity and Chemis "Tree" (we actually named a tree on top of a hill in our stadium the Chemis"Tree"). It served as a reminder to our players to keep changing and growing as a family. 2015 was the year that truly prepared us for the historic success we experienced the following year. We finished 8–5 again; however, the record doesn't tell the whole story. This was not an average team. This team played three championship teams to start the season, #1 Ohio State, #4 Michigan State, and Georgia Southern, who won the Sun Belt conference the year prior. We lost all three games. After those losses, I told our team that they had a chance to finish the year as champions. What this schedule taught us was that to be a champion, you must play champions. You must know what a champion plays like, looks like, hits like, and connects like. We did learn and we lost to all three. However, we learned from our past to create our future. This is an example of failing (going 0–3 in those games) creating growth!

The most important game of the year was our last game of the regular season. We were 6–5 at the time, heading to play #23 ranked Toledo in Toledo. WMU had NEVER beaten a Top 25 team. We knew it would be a battle and needed to find a way to make sure our team was locked in. I called my dear friend Becky Burleigh, the national championship women's soccer coach at the University of Florida, for some brainstorming motivation tactics. Based on that conversation, on Tuesday of that week I had every player write on a golf ball in black Sharpie marker the three hardest things that they had to "row" through in their lives and write them down within 15 seconds, because if it doesn't come to you in 15 seconds it must not have been life changing. We then put all the golf balls into a clear bucket to keep at practice every day. Players would ask all the time what the balls were for and I wouldn't tell anyone. I just kept saying that we need to look at our past to create our future and *row now*!

On Saturday, game day, we finished warming up and went into the locker room for the pregame speech. I pulled out the clear bucket of golf balls the players had been asking about all week. I told them that WMU had *never* beaten a Top 25 team. I then described the history of the golf ball. The first golf balls were smooth all the way around, but they took on small dents when golfers hit them hard. At the time, the dents were considered a bad thing. However, as golfers learned that the ball traveled farther with more dimples, it changed people's perspectives. As the design evolved, golf balls were given more and more dimples. Nowadays a golf ball has anywhere between 300 and 500 dimples.

"What does that mean?" I asked the team. They weren't sure, so I explained that all the things they wrote down on those golf balls were experiences they once saw as bad, as dents in their lives. All 450 difficult events they collectively experienced as a team, allowed us to go further and be here today in that moment, ready to do something this program had never done. Their past was ready to change their future.

"Now let's go take this further!" After a loud uproar, we took the field. We got our very first Top 25 win against Toledo that day, 35–30. After our players poured Gatorade over my head, they immediately ran to grab those golf balls that had been on our sideline the entire time and they carried them around like trophies. We went on to finish second in the West Division. We ended the season with the first ever bowl championship for WMU in school history by beating Middle Tennessee State University in the Popeye's Bahamas Bowl. We were able to take what we learned from the beginning of the season, losing to the three champions, and use that to become champions ourselves. Now people were able to see the framework going up atop the foundation.

The Windows Year

Our fourth year at WMU, 2016, was our "windows" year. We weren't a secret. People noticed us and expected us to be good. They could see into our "house" and were watching what we were doing. We weren't going to come out of nowhere to beat teams. Every publication had the WMU Broncos winning the MAC championship. There was a lot of outside noise, expectation, and pressure. We had to keep the vision looking out the window clearer than what people saw looking in. This meant our internal expectations had to be greater than the external expectations. We knew as a team that we had a target on our back. Row the Boat was now all over town. Stores, restaurants, bars, homes, basements, and more all had RTB fever. When we arrived at WMU we said that we wanted people to love us for our culture and our lifestyle of serving and giving and not just for winning. We knew this team had a chance—not guaranteed, but a chance to be special. We were now at a point where the players were leading, holding one another accountable and living the culture academically, athletically, socially, and spiritually. It was a connected team rowing in the same direction, at the same speed and with the same efficiency.

One of our central themes to the year was "grow higher." In order to achieve what we wanted to accomplish, we knew we couldn't stop growing. We used the bamboo tree as a symbol of growth. As a team, we studied the bamboo tree and noted things such as taking two to three years for the root system to form and then in one year, the tree can spring up to 90 feet. This team could go from 8–5 and winning the first bowl championship in school history in 2015 to untold heights in 2016.

We started out the season 3-0 defeating two Big Ten opponents, Northwestern University and the University of Illinois. Most media outlets now projected us to play in a New Year's Six bowl at the end of the year. There was a lot of football left to be played, and we had to keep our team rowing in the present while empowering them to be confident, yet also relaxed. We addressed, processed, and talked about the outside expectations and pressure we faced and made sure we created an inside-out, not outside-in, approach. We focused on ourselves, not the media or the fans. Weekly themes were applied to each game to keep our players loose and having fun while still addressing the importance of what they wanted to accomplish. I dressed up as a pirate one week, a shark another week, had Derek Jeter stop by and give away a scholarship to one of our players, and even had the coaches wear head to toe 1960s sports gear (bike coaching shorts, fishnet hats, pulled-up knee-high striped socks) to relive the championship days at WMU. We were just going to be us, the *real* us, and nobody could break our bond. We even had an opponent burn an oar on the sideline—literally. We beat that team 41–0. *Nobody* burns our oar. The only voices that mattered were the ones heard inside our walls.

As the season went on, we went 4–0, 5–0, 6–0. The pressure mounted; 7–0, 8–0, 9–0, and more pressure; 10–0, 11–0, and then finally the last game of the regular season against Toledo. If we beat Toledo, we'd go 12–0, win the MAC West division and go to Detroit for the MAC championship game. If we lost, we wouldn't win the West, we wouldn't go to Detroit, and we'd get knocked out of the national rankings. All that week we played the music from *Jaws* in the building to remind ourselves that the other players were coming for us because of what happened the year before, and remember *not* to let up. Sharks are always hungry, always attacking, and never full. They must constantly be moving forward and they never let up. I dressed up as a shark during practice to emphasize the theme and that any let up would allow this special season

49

to fade away. We ended up winning the game in front of a sold-out stadium with the fans constantly yelling and chanting "Row the Boat" all game. It felt like a lifetime away from the days when people said we couldn't and we wouldn't.

We went on to win the MAC championship with RTB chants throughout Ford Field. We were then selected to play Wisconsin in a New Year's Six bowl game. We were the 15th ranked team in the nation and heading to the Goodyear Cotton Bowl, one of the most historic bowl games in the history of college football. Even though we lost that game, the community of Kalamazoo saw what we were all capable of. We finished the season 13–1 with the highest GPA in school history. Numerous players were drafted into the NFL, including Top 5 pick Corey Davis. Many signed as free agents as well. ESPN College GameDay came to WMU when we hosted Buffalo. We won a conference championship. We established a brand and increased awareness for the great city of Kalamazoo. We witnessed kids' lives being changed forever by our community service in the hospitals and saw what's possible when people believe in the impossible. When people looked into our windows, they saw champions. When we looked out, we saw all the goals we accomplished. We had come a long way from year one, from people laughing at RTB to people chanting it. I will forever be proud of that team. Row the Boat proved to be very powerful. When put into practice, the philosophy, the principles, and the components create unstoppable energy. In this spirit I'm sure you are interested in learning more about what Row the Boat is all about.

Chapter 6

The Three Key Components of Row the Boat

P.J. Fleck

Row the Boat

The Oar

 The oar is the *energy* of your life— your mission and your purpose. It is the symbol of strength in the RTB culture. *You* choose whether your oar is in the water or whether you take it out and decide not to use it. Whether it's windy, raining, and stormy, or a calm, beautiful, sunny day, you decide to row or not. The oar is the only tool that moves the boat. This isn't a sailboat or a motorboat; without the oar, the boat does not move forward. *You* are the captain of your boat. *You* dictate to where and how fast to go. If you stop rowing, your life comes to a standstill. Just as the oar needs to be in the water for the boat to move, you must immerse yourself in life to live it to the fullest. Your energy is contagious and the energy you invest and share with others determines the quality of your life. When using the oar, there will be times when rowing is extremely hard, and will require intense, powerful work. At other times, efficiency—the smarter-not-harder approach—will be utilitzed in a calculated way to navigate through life.

Our RTB lifestyle is about two things: serving and giving. The oar allows us to share our program with our community, university, state, and country and to let others know we are rowing with them. In our football facility and stadium, oars from everywhere hang on the walls. The beautiful thing is that each oar has its own story to tell. Every spring, we encourage our fans to drop off personalized oars that we hang in the tunnel of our stadium. These oars usually represent lost loved ones, adversity, illness, or other trying times. We hear a lot of stories that touch our hearts and impact our program. These oars, the energy from our community, are the last thing our players see as they take the field on game day.

We also send out oars to people who let us know their story, struggle, and battles. Each oar has a certain color that represents a particular challenge or cause. Pink oars are for breast cancer. Puzzle piece oars are for autism awareness. Red oars are for heart disease. We even have yellow oars for troops that come home to our community. We want our fans, community, alumni, and others to know that we are rowing right along with them and that the people in our program can make a *huge* difference in the lives of others. The oar has become a powerful symbol of the energy we all possess to make a difference.

The Boat

 The boat represents *sacrifice*. This analogy is as simple as it gets. The more you serve, give, and make your life about helping others, the better and more fulfilled your life will be. The more you do this, the bigger your boat gets. Little boats don't go very far or carry many people. They sink in big storms. Big boats go a long way, carry more people, and can handle the biggest storms.

I have realized that when adverse situations happen in my life, the only way to truly feel any better is to serve and give somehow, in some way. The more you sacrifice in your life and give to others, the stronger your life and boat become.

Listening to, looking for, and lifting up those around you to make them better builds a stronger boat.

Row the Boat is not about focusing on yourself. It's about rowing through life to be great for others and to help others be their best. No one rows through life alone, so the boat represents a group of people all rowing together. When the group is rowing with a common focus, intention, mission, and purpose, the group becomes a team and the team becomes unstoppable. The more you serve others, the bigger your boat gets and the larger your team becomes. Your impact expands and more people decide to row with you. This doesn't happen overnight, but as your boat and your impact grow, your life becomes more rewarding. We teach our players that they should never be a better football player than they are a person. Sacrifice is the key to fulfillment.

The Compass

The compass is the *direction,* the beacon to help take us from where we are to where we dream of going. The vision we have for our lives, how we speak to ourselves, and the people we surround ourselves with help create this dream. If you want to be a doctor, tell yourself you can be a doctor and find a way to be around doctors. If you want to be a coach, tell yourself you can be a coach and get around coaches. If you want to heal from a hardship you are going through, tell yourself you can and then spend time with others who have been through and have overcome the same struggle.

A boat race has a finish line you are rowing toward. In life there is no finish line. The dream is the journey and the journey is the dream. You have to just keep rowing. You don't get a perfect set of plans. Rather, life gives you a north star and other people to join you on your journey. From mentors, you learn how to become who you want to be. From friends, you learn how to give and receive in a relationship. From those who are struggling, you learn how to practice empathy. From those who are enjoying success, you learn how to celebrate others. From those who want to give up, you learn how to give encouragement. From others' mistakes, you learn what you don't want, and from your heroes, you learn what you do want. The people in your life help point you in the direction you want to go. Wherever you are headed in life, you need direction, belief in yourself, and other people to help you get there. The compass is your tool to move forward on that path.

Chapter 7

A Bigger Opportunity and Challenge

Jon Gordon

58

Row the Boat

The Row the Boat principles are powerful. P.J. utilized them to turn around the WMU football program and become a top team in the nation. At the Cotton Bowl, chants of "Row the Boat" coming from the WMU crowd—which outsold Wisconsin in tickets—brought it full circle. A community and fan base that once thought RTB was just a slogan had now adopted it as a lifestyle. Oars, cardboard boats, compass signs, and a contagious spirit spread throughout the city like never before. People who once doubted, feared, and mocked RTB now understood that if they changed their mindset, directed their energy toward one common goal, sacrificed and put others before themselves, led with purpose, and never gave up, they would accomplish something they never had before. That 13–1 championship season and Cotton Bowl experience proved that the RTB style could work in every area of life for players, coaches, business leaders, workers, and anyone else who applied its principles.

It worked once in Kalamazoo, Michigan. But could it work at the Power 5 Big Ten level? As a result of this success, P.J. was hired by the University of Minnesota to become their new head football coach. Minnesota was dealing with a player boycott and a sexual assault case at the time P.J. was hired. Minnesota hadn't been to the Rose Bowl since 1962 and hadn't won a Big Ten championship since 1967.

Everyone wondered if P.J. could do what he did at Western Michigan again. Were he and Row the Boat just a one-hit wonder? Would Row the Boat also work at the University of Minnesota? Just because it worked at WMU didn't mean it would necessarily work again. It's hard to quantify and measure culture and principles. So many factors determine

A Bigger Opportunity and Challenge

whether a team or organization succeeds. However, having worked with countless sports teams in college and the pros and with numerous Fortune 500 companies, I can tell you that leadership, culture, values, and principles are what drives a team and organization to success. Great leaders who lead by a core set of principles and values and build a great culture create success wherever they go.

Thus, if P.J. and Row the Boat were a key part of an organization's success equation, we would see a pattern of success wherever P.J. went. Did that happen at the University of Minnesota? P.J. Fleck and RTB would be put to the test. Let's find out how it went.

Chapter 8

Rowing the Boat at the University of Minnesota

P. J. Fleck

62

Row the Boat

A Culture in Need of Change

After the Cotton Bowl, I was getting ready to sign a brand-new deal to keep me at WMU. Heather and I made a rule. We truly wouldn't consider taking a different job until after the Cotton Bowl. Many jobs did not like this because they wanted me to immediately start recruiting, fundraising, and team building. There was no way we were *not* going to coach in that bowl game. Our players and staff gave everything they had to get us to a special bowl game and I needed to give them all I had and finish the season with them.

We continued to *row* and coach our team for the biggest game of WMU's history. After the Cotton Bowl I was asked where I'd be going after the game. I told everyone I was headed back to WMU, and that's what I intended to do. The schools that showed interest had hired their coaches already and I came to the conclusion that we were going to stay at WMU for a long while. A few days later I got a call from Mark Coyle, the brilliant AD at the University of Minnesota, asking if I was interested in the newly opened job in the Twin Cities. The job hadn't been available for long and I didn't really know much about Minnesota. But I did know what happened and why the job was open. According to Mark Coyle, the culture needed to be changed, and I was his pick to get that done.

As I previously mentioned, I define change and "truth listening" and culture as "positively connecting people." That's what I was being hired to do: truly listen and connect this team in a positive way with a new lifestyle approach of never giving up and serving and giving. I would find out the challenge would be very similar to years prior, but this time on a grander and more public stage.

63

The Harder Right

Prior to taking the job, Heather asked me two questions. First, "Are you ready for another year one?" When you are 13–1 in year four, you sometimes forget what year one (1–11) felt like. You knew you did it, but you sometimes forget the daily row and storms that came your way. The past is fogged out by recent success.

Second, Heather asked me, "Does it scare you to go to Minnesota?" She had asked me this question for other jobs as well, but this answer was very different. I didn't want my next job to be just a job; I wanted it to be more of a calling. It needed to be a place where we could create a life, not just make a living. I wanted it to be a place where we could make an impact that could be legendary both on and off the field. I wanted to unite our program, players, and staff with our city and affect people of all ages, even the ones who weren't interested in football. I wanted our city to feel like it was *their* program and grow to love our RTB culture and admire how we lived our lives on and off the field. I wanted to be the coach who could bring what our alums deserve so much: championships. So my answer to Heather's question, "Does Minnesota scare you?" was "*Absolutely!*" She followed it up with, "Then we are going to Minnesota. You will make your biggest impact where it will be the hardest."

When having this conversation with Heather, the Cadet's Prayer came to mind. Mike Sullivan, my offensive coordinator when I coached for the Tampa Bay Buccaneers, used to recite it to our team: "Make us to choose the harder right instead of the easier wrong, and never to be content with a half-truth when the whole can be won." The Minnesota football team was divided. RTB was coming to connect everyone!

Minnesota's football program is actually one of the most storied in college football, claiming seven national championships and 18 Big Ten championships. However, Minnesota's last Big Ten championship was back in 1967, 13 years before I was even born. The last national championship was in 1960. The one and only Heisman trophy was won by Bruce Smith, not the defensive end from the Buffalo Bills but a halfback from 1941. I was going to connect this "Ski-U-Mah" tradition with the present and restore Minnesota to what it could be. You can start to see the familiar pattern. It was my kind of job, but everyone around me was telling me to wait for a "better" job. There were so many things that hadn't been accomplish in a very long time at Minnesota. Some would call this hard, risky, and a questionable move. However, people are what make a place the right place—the kind of people who stop making excuses. I was going to bring in people who focus on how they could do something instead of why they couldn't do something. The type of people who transform teams, organizations, communities, and cities. RTB would now be able to reach millions instead of hundreds of thousands and have the opportunity to make a greater impact, touch more lives, and influence a major city.

Another Year One: The Dig

In my first team meeting, with a majority of the players connected through Facebook Live, I'm not sure how many actually wanted to be there. All the year one memories flooded my brain. This is what Heather meant about year one. These players didn't care if I was two-time Coach of the Year in the MAC or had just led one of the most historic seasons in college football for a team not part of the Power Five. They didn't care about the highest GPA in WMU history and RTB being a staple in changing a community. The team I was inheriting had just almost boycotted their bowl game.

The team was divided and had many sides. Some wanted to boycott; others were indifferent. Some wanted change; others did not. They wanted to know why I was there, what I could do for them, and how this RTB thing was going to affect their lives. Period. The uphill battle was underway— again. It was time for another dig. We knew there would be an enormous number of challenges with what we were going to implement. We knew storms would come from players, opponents, faculty, administrators, alumni, donors, media, critics, community, fans, and old staff members inside the program trying to sabotage and influence the daily agendas and the current players so that we wouldn't succeed. Whether due to budgetary concerns, our drug-testing policy, or that we ask our players sit up front in class with a collared shirt to show professors they were there and actually cared what instructors had to say, we knew there would be critics of how we ran our program. We knew that having practice in the morning so our players could dedicate their afternoons to academics would ruffle some feathers in the faculty. We knew that having RTB as our new culture would make some fans, alumni, and supporters uneasy because our tradition was already established with Ski-U-Mah (our rally cry). We knew that with the recent wins Minnesota had, it would be hard to change players' perspectives because in a lot of their minds they won six or eight games a year and just won their bowl game they had been threatening to boycott. So why change anything? I told our players in that first team meeting that I chose them, they didn't choose me. I made a promise to all of them that this culture would change their lives in a positive way both on and off the field. I borrowed a quote from the great Bo Schembechler and told them "those who stay will be champions."

Setting the Standard

Our team's reputation was important. Socially, we knew we had to change the mindset of how players looked at themselves off the field and how they were perceived on campus by faculty and other students. The new standards had to be set high enough in all four areas of our lives—academically, athletically, socially, and spiritually—to see who truly wanted to be here. Yet at the same time we wanted to create the most optimistic, empathetic, creative player-led program we could put together. You have one year to set the standard of the culture and that culture can never, ever be compromised. If a player missed class, he didn't play. It may sound harsh, but if we were ever going to get the *right* people to play in our program, they would have to value their whole life as a *student* athlete. How you do one thing is how you do everything, and you must do it all at an elite level. The standard was clearly set in all areas. *It was time to row.*

A Culture of Rowers

One of the first people I met when I got to the University of Minnesota was a young man, who has now become a household name, Casey O'Brien. I was sitting in my office shortly after arriving at UM when a knock at the door and a simple "Hey Coach Fleck, you got a second?" changed my life forever. I had no idea who this kid was. My first reaction to, "Wow, here's a kid on my team who is genuinely happy I'm here and has an energetic voice and a mission in life." I couldn't help wondering when more of these guys on our team would show up.

But as we talked, I discovered he wasn't actually on our team! Damn—the one guy I could use as an example of the *how* and the *oar* and the *energy* was not even one of my players. But the good news was that he *wanted* to be on the team.

I couldn't say yes fast enough. This was the personality, the mental makeup, and the approach to life with which to build a culture and team. Lots of people each year want to join a football team at the Big Ten level, but Casey was different. His energy and optimism were contagious. I fell in love with his passion and spirit so fast, maybe because I was just looking for one person to buy in and he was it. He knew all about us from WMU, and he knew a lot of the same people I knew as well.

I asked Casey what position he wanted to play and he said holder. I had never heard that one before. Holder, seriously? There had to be more to why he just wanted to be a holder. I realized that all the people Casey and I both knew were involved with children's hospitals. Why? Because Casey was a two-time cancer survivor at the time, five-time by his graduation in 2020. In that moment, I was talking to one of the players who would change my life forever and let me know by a wink from God that I was exactly where I needed to be. Whether we won or lost, God had us exactly where he needed us. Any doubts I had about taking this job ended right then. It took me two seconds to tell Casey O'Brien he was on the team. In that moment, I knew we were both called to be there. I found myself a Rower, and the legacy of RTB and Casey O'Brien began that day.

We finished the 2017 season 5–7 with two conference wins. The record wasn't as important as making sure our players knew that everything and anything we ever did as coaches and as a program was *always* for our players! We possibly could have won more games, but creating the culture was more important than winning, and we couldn't let

69

anything compromise that. We hold our players to a high standard not just because we want them to be elite players, but more importantly because we want them to be elite husbands, fathers, brothers, and sons one day. To beat teams that had 50 or more four-star players while we only had 5 four-star players, our culture needed to be stronger than just our skill on the field. We had to recruit and develop overachievers (Kings of the Toos). I knew they were just right for us! I also called them "roWErs"—guys who would Row the Boat and help us create an elite program.

A Roller Coaster Season: The Foundation

2018, our second year at Minnesota, was a make-or-break year for RTB once again. Having only won five games without playing in a bowl game when they won eight games and a bowl game the year before I arrived made a lot of people question Row the Boat. It was going to be an important and challenging year. After a 5–7 start in year one, we had to propel this program forward. We signed one of the highest-ranked classes in Minnesota's history. The challenge was that most of the young players were going to have to play right away. We would end up being the youngest team in college football in 2018. This is *not* an ideal thing when it involves a lot of young men playing against grown men in the Big Ten. However, every single player on the field that year truly wanted to be there. You win a lot more with a team that *wants* and *needs* to be there instead of feeling like they *have to* be there. We knew we weren't going to be the strongest, fastest, or most experienced team in the country, so we had to give them something obtainable to reach. We told our team that we needed to become the most mature team. We defined reaching maturity as the point when doing what you have to do becomes what you want to do.

After a 3–0 start, we lost four straight games before defeating Indiana to stand at 4–4 on the season. Our next game was against Illinois and the week leading up to it was the deciding factor in how the rest of the season would play out. During the week we held a funeral inside of TCF Bank Stadium. Nick Connelly, one of our offensive lineman, had succumbed to his battle with cancer earlier in the season. Talk about a swing of emotions: calm seas one day, hurricane the next. One moment we were on top of the world from a win; the next we were having a funeral for one of our fallen brothers. Remember, these are young men, not adults dealing with this. Some say you remember the plays and wins the most in coaching. I don't agree with that. I remember the *people, moment, and memories,* and what they taught me along the way.

This team was about to fail the most to grow the most. The boat—along with its captain—was about to be tested with decisions that would change the course of our program. We were going to Champaign, Illinois, for the ninth game of the year. We were big favorites in the Illinois game. With a win we would be 5–4, with three games left and a bowl game within our sights.

The game didn't go according to plan. We got beat at Illinois 55–31. It wasn't just a loss; it was a thumping. Our team was flat. We were just going through the motions on both sides of the ball, and especially on defense. It made sense that

Nick's funeral affected our team, but I saw something I hadn't seen before in my team that I was never going to accept: quitting. I saw the team quit and I knew at that moment that a change of leadership was needed on the defensive side.

The next day I made a change to the staff on defense and promoted Joe Rossi to interim defensive coordinator. Joe is one of the best coaches, fathers, teachers, and husbands I have ever met. I didn't know if the move would be permanent; however, it was a way for me to see how the same defense that had been so successful in years past would play under new leadership. If the defense played poorly under Joe Rossi, then maybe it was time for a different defensive scheme. If the defense improved, only a change in leadership was required. We would learn a lot in the next three weeks.

After the Illinois loss, we crushed Purdue to improve our record to 5–5 and had a stellar defensive performance. We then lost to Northwestern (the Big Ten West champs that year) to move to 5–6 and had to now play Wisconsin, at Camp Randall in Madison, where our program hadn't won since 1994. The University of Minnesota hadn't beaten Wisconsin anywhere for 14 straight years! So the task before us was not easy, but this is how legendary teams and programs start. Monumental wins create energy and enable the program to take off. If you don't get the big wins, it can lead to the boat sinking. When building a program, time is not a coach's best friend. Nowadays, if you don't turn around a program quickly you may be quickly out of a job.

Before the game, I knew I had to say something I had never said before. The talk *had* to be different. I had to make sure they knew they could win and should win, and *they* were the team to end the losing streak. I had to make sure they knew what this win would mean to our program, city, and state. When I arrived at Minnesota all I was told was, "Coach, just beat Wisconsin and you can stay here forever," "Please get us the Axe back." You could tell how thirsty our fans were to end the streak in college football's most played rivalry and bring Paul Bunyan's Axe back to Minnesota. (For those not familiar with the details of the Minnesota–Wisconsin rivalry, the seven-foot Axe is the trophy awarded to the winner.)

So what did I say? To start with, right before we departed for Madison the day before the game, I gave each player making the trip a bottle of Axe body spray. I told them we would celebrate with it in the locker room after the game. I wanted them to *believe* they could get the win. I was preparing in the locker room before I talked to my team and I kept going over what I wanted to say to them. I had it all written out, word for word. However, with one minute to go before I addressed them, I told myself, the hell with it. I'm going to just tell them how I feel from my heart. That's when the words I had never said before came out. I told them, "Do *not* be afraid, men. Do *not* be afraid to become a *legend*." If we won this game, it would arguably mean more to our state, city, and university than anything we accomplished on the field in the last 25 years. To lose to your border-state rival 15 years in a row and to know that kids in our city who were 15 years old had *never* seen Minnesota beat Wisconsin meant that winning this game would be legendary.

Not only did our guys Row the Boat that day, but they rowed like they had never rowed before. Victory would become ours. We will never forget that 37–15 victory and Camp Randall

Rowing the Boat at the University of Minnesota

Stadium being empty with the exception of Gopher fans with time still on the clock. We spent about an hour on the field celebrating with the Axe together. When we got to the locker room, all of the players jubilantly sprayed their Axe body spray in the air. It was the smell of victory and one that will always be remembered by our staff and the players on that team. Lost in all the excitement, we had won our sixth game and become bowl eligible. Wisconsin was who we were wanting to become. Barry Alvarez created something at Wisconsin that was very special. Years ago, I asked Barry a question at an AFCA convention when I was a first-year head coach at WMU: "How did you do it at Wisconsin?" He said simply, "We stopped making excuses." Noted! *No* excuses, only reasons why we can, not why we can't.

We became legends for that day and cemented our place in the Gophers history books with that monumental, streak-ending win. It was our turn to have the Axe back, and we shared it with the entire state. Over the next year the Axe was rented out daily for birthday parties, weddings, anniversaries, parties, and alumni events. It was once again ours. We reached maturity toward the end of year and Joe Rossi was hired as our new DC in the locker room right after that win! The win at Wisconsin, combined with a Quick Lane Bowl championship over Georgia Tech, was a fitting end to a roller-coaster year with the youngest team in the country. It was very clear the foundation for RTB at Minnesota had hardened.

Rest-OAR-Ation: The Framework

Our third year at Minnesota, 2019, would go down in the history books as one of the greatest seasons in Gopher history for a lot of reasons. We used the concept "Rest-OAR-ation" because we thought this team could bring back the winning feeling that Gopher football fans and alumni had in the 1930s, '40s, '50s, and '60s. Coming off a 7–6 record and a Bowl victory over Georgia Tech, the internal pressure and expectation was high with mostly everyone coming back. However, the predictions from the media and "experts" had us picked as low as sixth in the West, and for good reason. We were still going to be one of the youngest teams in America and had not won a championship in over 50 years. However, we would not let someone else tell us how far our boat could go. It didn't matter what they thought. What mattered was what we believed and did. We had dreams, hopes, and aspirations of winning it all. We were doing everything at a national championship level, period. The season was a test of how much we had learned about Rowing the Boat, and the tests came quickly.

We were supposed to win the first three games by double digits, yet we won all three by a combined total of 13 points and needed to Row the Boat in every way. After a come from behind victory over FCS powerhouse South Dakota State in our opener, we traveled to Fresno State. The year prior we beat them in a hard fought game on a last second interception in the end zone by Antoine Winfield Jr. (who, in 2021, got his team to "Row" in the end zone during the Super Bowl after he recorded an interception that sealed the victory). We would beat Fresno State in a similar fashion this year. We had a 4th-and-goal from the 17-yard line and had to score a touchdown just to send the game into overtime. With seconds to spare, our third wide receiver that season, Chris Autman-Bell, caught a perfect vertical route thrown by Tanner Morgan to send the game into overtime. In the second overtime, Antoine Winfield Jr. intercepted a pass to end the game. It was like déjà vu.

75

The following week we returned to TCF Bank Stadium to play Georgia Southern. Late in the game, we faced a 3rd-and-30 from our own 6-yard line. We were down by 4 points with just 2:54 left in the game. Talk about a storm and rocky sea with a boat struggling to stay afloat. It was time for one of our less heralded players to make an impact. Demetrius Douglas, who ran a hitch route, caught the ball and ran for a gain of about 22 yards. Now it was 4th-and-8. If we didn't get this next 1st down, the game was over and we would lose to Georgia Southern.

At this time most of the crowd had left because in their mind there was no possible way we could pick up 3rd-and-30. The old-timer fans were thinking about the past and how the Gophers never win these games. But this team was different. This team knew how to keep *rowing*. We got the first down and then after a few more plays with 10 seconds to go, Tyler Johnson caught a fade in the end zone to win the game for the Gophers. Winning this game might have seemed impossible for most but not for the RTB culture. We were never out of it as long as we kept our oar in the water. I have that 3rd-and-30 picture in my office at work and at home to remind me that we are all never out of it.

After three consecutive thrilling wins, the boat reached some calmer waters. We handily won five straight Big Ten games in a row. You could see the connectivity and love within this team grow. This set up the most epic game in TCF Bank Stadium history.

The Penn State game was one of the highlights, if not the pinnacle, of my career to date in terms of winning a football game. Both teams were nationally ranked in the Top 15. Both teams were 8–0. It was the first sold-out crowd in close to

10 years for the Gophers. The night before the game I had each player use a silver Sharpie to write on a piece of coal the worst thing that happened to them in their lifetime, similar to what I did when I was at WMU and asked the players to write on a golf ball. I again gave them only 15 seconds to write because if you think too much about it, it doesn't transform you. Once all the coal pieces were written on, I had the players place them in a clear bucket and sent them to bed for the night. Before the game, during the pregame speech, I explained the science of how diamonds were made from the pressure of coal. How everything they had overcome makes them their best self, diamonds. I reached deep down into the bin and pulled out a huge diamond—plastic of course, but it looked real! I told them to go be diamonds today!

The game was a heavyweight matchup. We tested each other's resolve, rowing ability, persistence, response, and togetherness. We won the game when our true sophomore safety, Jordan Howden, intercepted a pass in the final seconds to secure the victory. What's great about Jordan ending the game with an interception in the end zone was that the year prior he was forced into starting due to an injury and it didn't go well for Jordan. He failed over and over again but he never quit and never took his oar out of the water. He went from failing a ton in 2018 to learning from it and becoming a *huge* success in 2019. Learning from your past to create your future is critical to building successful teams in sports and business.

Fans, alum, and families all stormed the field after the game. It was the first of our two wins against a Top 10 team and it was the first time we beat two Top 10 teams in the same season since 1956. It was a moment I had dreamed of and

Rowing the Boat at the University of Minnesota

one of the greatest moments I've had on the field as a coach. In the locker room afterward, we went to the bin of coal. I reminded them that the hardships in their own life and football life have made this moment possible. I reiterated that for diamonds to become diamonds, they need extreme pressure. And told them, "Men, you were diamonds today and will be forever because you row through your obstacles in life!"

We finished the regular season 10–2 with a share of the Big Ten West division title, but Wisconsin beat us and won the Axe back in the last game of the season, where we hosted ESPNs College GameDay. It wasn't the way we wanted it to end, but we were invited to play in the Outback Bowl against Auburn, who had just beaten Alabama a few weeks before. We saw this game as an experience that would prepare us to play for a national championship down the road. This was our time to show that we could beat one of the best traditional programs in the country on a national stage. We were about 10-point underdogs entering the game. One of our best offensive linemen was out with a broken leg and Auburn's first-round defensive lineman opted to play. This was going to be a huge challenge for us. Our offensive coordinator left to take the OC job at Penn State prior to the bowl game, so some of our staff were doing things for the first time, like interim offense coordinator Matt Simon. The message all week was that it would take all of us and *all* of our best performances as coaches and players to win the game.

The game was tight and, like many of our games that year, it came down to the last possession. We took the ball over with just under nine minutes left in the game and never gave it back to them. There was a fourth and one call near the end of the game. If we got the 1st down, we would almost be assured victory, but if we didn't get it, they would get the ball with an opportunity to tie the game in the final minute. I heard the call come over the headset from Matt Simon and I immediately called a timeout.

The call was for a play-action pass to a tight end who hadn't caught a pass all regular season. Bryce Witham had played a lot of football for us, but had battled injury after injury. In the most important call all year, when we needed only 1 yard, were we going to throw the ball to a guy who hadn't caught a pass that season? I asked Matt, "Is this what you want? Are you *sure?*" Matt immediately replied, *"Absolutely!"* When I heard that said with extreme conviction, I asked our team if we wanted to go for it. Without hesitation they too said, *"Absolutely!"*

After that, there was no way we wouldn't get that 1st down. We had come too far not to finish it. This had become a player-led elite team right before our eyes. The play worked and Bryce Witham caught the ball that was thrown behind him with one hand to move us closer to victory. After picking up one more 1st down, the game was over! It took us all Rowing the Boat in the same direction with the same speed and efficiency to beat a heavyweight like Auburn with more than 50 four-star recruits and numerous first-rounders and *we did it!* For those three hours on that day, *we* were the better team. And we restored the winning football tradition at Minnesota. That 2019 team accomplished 82 firsts in our over-130-year history, including:

1. AP Top 10 win in a bowl game

2. Won the Outback Bowl

3. 7 Big Ten wins

4. Highest rank in CFP poll history (#8)

5. 53 Academic All Big Ten (3.21 team GPA)

6. 17 Players named to All Big Ten teams

7. 86 players above a 3.0

Along with 116 Rest-OAR-ations:

1. Started season 9–0 (first time since 1904)

2. Won 4 Big Ten games by at least 20 points (first time since 1934)

3. Won January 1 bowl game (first time since 1962)

4. Won 2 games against Top 10 opponents (first time since 1956)

5. 10 regular season wins (first time since 1905)

6. 11-win season (first time since 1904)

7. Finished ranked in Top 10 (first time since 1962)

8. Highest in season rank (#7, first time since 1962)

This team was one for the ages. A team that *rowed* their way to victory so many times because they didn't give up, rowed *together* through chaos, and did it *for* so many, including themselves. Casey O'Brien guided the leadership on how to row, not only by surviving cancer for the fifth time but by fulfilling his dream of playing in a college football game when he entered the game against Rutgers as the holder! The one player who first believed in RTB led us the entire year with his personal battle showing us *all* how to Row the Boat!

Chapter 9

A Wave of Change

Jon Gordon

82

Row the Boat

P.J. and I decided to write this book before we had any idea that the worldwide coronavirus pandemic was coming our way. The University of Minnesota football team had just won 11 games for the first time since 1904. P.J. and Row the Boat have turned around a struggling program once again and it looked like he and his team were about to become a national championship contender. The University of Minnesota football program was on the rise and, like most of us, was getting ready to have an incredible 2020. And then COVID-19 hit.

What started out as a ripple from the other side of the world wound up rocking the boat and brought a tumultuous wave of change that greatly impacted college football and P.J.'s program, as well as every aspect of society. Several of UM's best players opted out of the season for pandemic safety concerns. When players tested positive, it affected who could play and how many could play on any given Saturday. It was a season filled with change and adversity that would truly test P.J., his team, and the Row the Boat principles.

As I watched the season unfold, I wondered how P.J. and his team were doing. He and his staff were used to rising each year, winning more and more games, not rising and then falling. How would Row the Boat adjust and work in this situation? A true test of someone's principles and philosophies is whether they adhere to them regardless of circumstances. It would have been easy to say let's publish this book only after P.J. wins a national championship, but that's not what P.J. and Row the Boat are all about, and it's why I love both what they stand for and what they believe. Row the Boat is not just about creating a successful culture and program and winning championships. It's also about how you handle adversity when a wave of change rocks your boat to the core of your existence. With this in mind, let's learn from P.J. how you can keep rowing through adversity and through waves of change.

Chapter 10

Rowing through Adversity

P.J. Fleck

86

Row the Boat

Responding to Adversity

"Life happens" applies equally to sports, business, and life. It's how we respond to a circumstance that makes our organization and team who we are and determines where will be heading. The path to success will constantly be filled with peaks and valleys and everyone, without exception, will experience them. The vision we have for our life, career, team, family, or organization doesn't take into account the natural pitfalls that *will* come. When they come, we will deal with them at that time. Issues and challenges always arise as you rise and fall and rise again on your way to realizing your vision. Whoever is better able to handle adverse moments and periods will get ahead. Whoever fails at this will fall behind.

You must remember that the dream is the *journey*, not the destination. Every hard day, every loss, every lost family member, every financial burden, every "no," every divorce or breakup, every hardship is part of *your* journey on the way to achieve your dream and is meant to teach you how to handle success and failure. These tests help you build leather skin for the assignments in your life. Have you ever had something happen to you that seemed devastating at the time, but when you looked back later in life you realized that it shaped what and who you are as a person? This doesn't mean it's easy to handle when you are going through it. But it does mean that if we keep rowing, we will see that the success is the journey itself, rather than a particular destination.

I love when players tell me they want to "make it" to the NFL. I ask, "Just make it there? One day? One week? Play in one game? Play a year? Make it to a second contract? Be an All-Pro? Be a Hall of Famer? Be the greatest ever? What's the dream specifically?" There will be a major price to pay during that journey, and it is definitely not filled with calm seas all the time. In fact, the journey is mostly filled with storms. Is the dream worth it, and can you keep rowing through those times?

Just as not everyone looks at the journey and life the same way, not everyone will row the same way. Not every boat is the same, and the water is different depending on where you are in your journey. Some will row harder, and some will row in a different direction. Some will lose sight of their vision. One of the key elements of your journey is surrounding yourself with people who want to go to the same destination. Only by rowing together can we achieve our goals.

Storms affect people differently, and 2020 certainly brought us heavy storms. COVID-19, social injustice, the political divide, and the election all affected people in various ways. Yet, regardless of the differences, we were *all* affected by that tumultuous year. You could not hide from it. You had to face it. Each of us made daily choices to row or quit rowing. In challenging times we could either think of others with empathy or just think about ourselves and how it affected us. We could live a life of serving, giving, and learning or choose to ignore the lessons we were being presented with. We could choose to avoid discussing difficult topics, or we could have the difficult conversations we needed to have as a team and a society in order to learn and grow together. In order to successfully navigate the waters of 2020, we would need to live with a compass of faith.

Compass of Faith

Nothing in 2020 was predictable, organized, or regimented. We all had to adapt to changing tides and winds. New "norms" were established. To a coach, a schedule is everything, and we had no schedule. Just like the rest of the word, there were times we couldn't leave our homes and instantly our homes became our offices, and Zoom calls became our normal way to hold meetings. We could only have so many people in a room at one time. Many of our staff and their spouses had to become teachers at home. We saw many families being separated for months because of flight restrictions and quarantining. Those in the medical community risked their lives daily, while many others had to deal with the pain of not being able to see their sick loved ones in hospitals. Too many died alone with no visitors to ease the pain or to comfort them in their suffering.

I acutely felt for the patients in the children's hospitals that were accustomed to the many visitors that helped brighten their days. Now they were restricted to being visited by just a single family member.

In the realm of football, we saw canceled seasons, opt-outs, canceled games, and experienced the anxiety of Q-tips being jammed up our noses daily and the stress-filled 15 minutes before you found out whether you had contracted a virus that could harm you. We recruited players to come to our school whom we had never met and who had never even visited the school before.

Where was the safe and reliable place we all had in our lives? There was no playbook for this. However, if we set our compass to faith, we had a chance to get through this and become stronger and better than before. If we complained and worried only about ourselves, loneliness, depression, and anger would take over. Whoever could keep rowing no matter what came their way had a chance to make it through 2020 with an elite vision and focus for 2021. For me and our team it was about having faith that all that happened to us in the big storm of 2020 was there to teach us and prepare us to create a better world tomorrow.

The Ultimate Response

In 2020, the game that would define our Row the Boat response to all the change and adversity we had been through was when we played against Nebraska. We were down 33 players (the majority being COVID-related) playing in Lincoln, where the Gophers had only won one time since 1960. We were 9.5-point underdogs. We had around 20 freshmen playing and were playing to our third-string kicker. We overcame so much adversity, kept rowing, and won the game. It was a feat that could only happen with everyone rowing *for* each other. Winning that game might just be a quick memory for some and maybe will be forgotten by many, but that game ball is going in a display case for what it meant to our Row the Boat culture. *Everyone* was needed for that cultural win!

It wasn't a championship season for us. We lost to Wisconsin in overtime the following week. We had a losing record after a historic winning season the year before. But I will never forget how our coaching staff, players, and program kept battling throughout the year and the season together. We kept fighting and despite being outmanned in almost every game we played we never gave up. We rowed the boat through adversity and demonstrated that we truly believed in the RTB principles no matter how difficult the circumstances. I know without a doubt that it had made us stronger and will prepare us for the future.

The year 2020 taught me five things that I will take with me forever:

1. Faith. Row the boat no matter how hard it gets. We had faith that 2020 was there to teach us how we could all grow more, do more, become more, and love more.

2. Empathy. Sacrifice for the person next to you. Serve them and their needs. Get to know who they are and their story. No matter our race, religion, or gender, we need to put ourselves in the shoes of others and learn, listen, and *act* to make a difference!

3. Unity. Together is the only way. You can't row by yourself. We all need one another—no hierarchy, no division, no ignorance. We can all row together and row *with* one another. Hold each other accountable and don't be afraid to have difficult conversations. Our compass is each other!

4. Gratitude. COVID-19 showed us how much we needed to appreciate our daily blessings by taking so many of them away. We need to be thankful for each other and take care of one another.

5. The standard will always be the standard. Circumstances will change and reasons for *not* upholding the standard of the culture will always exist. In drastic times of change this will be tested.

Chapter 11

Beyond Football

Jon Gordon

94

Row the Boat

When P.J. created Row the Boat, he had a vision to impact more than just his football program. He wanted to impact his university, community, state, country, and people from all walks of life. He wanted to make a difference beyond the football field and the locker room. He knew it started with him and his team, and that from inside the locker room and inside their minds and hearts they would have a ripple effect on the outside world.

So far, we've seen the impact Row the Boat has had on the teams and places P.J. has been. But I was also curious about the influence of Row the Boat on people beyond football. I asked P.J. to share with me some of his favorite stories of seeing Row the Boat utilized by people outside the football program.

Chapter 12

The Impact
of Row the Boat
Beyond Football

P.J. Fleck

98

Row the Boat

Helping Families Stay Together

Our players have done and continue to do so much work with the University of Minnesota Masonic Children's Hospital that it inspired Heather and me to start the Row the Boat Fleck Family Fund. It is designed to help families stay together and ease their burdens during their stay at the hospital. Our focus is to keep families together as much as possible so the focus can be on their children and their marriage. If the family is united and connected and less stressed, they can better handle the recovery and process in the hospital.

So many stressors come into play when your child is admitted to the hospital: financial stress, siblings' stress, marital stress, physiological stress. The RTB fund covers any cost that families incur staying together so they don't have to leave their child due to financial pressures.

Rowing Together

All our proceeds from any RTB merchandise go right to both Ronald McDonald House and the Row the Boat Fleck Family Fund at the children's hospital. We didn't create RTB to make money for ourselves. We came up with it to help others get through various storms in their lives and know that they are not alone in their journey. We did it to join forces with certain organizations to help raise more money and awareness for their causes and missions. Our football program and RTB has raised hundreds of thousands of dollars through the sale of RTB gear donations and sponsorships. We want the Gopher football team and RTB to be an elite example of what never giving up looks like, as well as never counting yourself out, no matter how bleak things might look. Our message and mission go way beyond football. We want our fans in the stands to know that when you are Rowing the Boat with our football team on Saturdays, rooting us to victory, you are also helping so many youngsters and their families, which is way bigger than the final score on the scoreboard! You don't have to play football, coach football, or even like football to Row the Boat. Just love your life, give your time and energy to others, give hope to all by staying connected in faith and life, and row on!

Row the Boat has affected so many over the years with such amazing help from the University of Minnesota Masonic Children's Hospital and all the people involved. One moment I'll never forget is when Braxton Battaglia, age 10, spoke to our team in 2019 before we left for the Outback Bowl. She also made the trip down to Tampa and was there in the stands for the celebration after we beat Auburn in one of the greatest wins in school history. Her exclamation before we got on the airplane to head down to Tampa will ring in the ears of our players forever: "If I can Row the Boat and beat cancer, then *you* can beat Auburn!" And we did and won the Outback Bowl to finish one of the greatest seasons in school history!

In 2017 Kyle Tanner gave away a scholarship to his favorite Gopher player Justin Juenemann (our third-string walk-on kicker at the time) during a team meeting. Kyle loved Justin so much because Justin visited him in the hospital weekly as he bravely fought and defeated cancer. This story has special meaning because Kyle was a Central Michigan graduate, the rival of Western Michigan where I coached from 2013 to 2016.

So he was definitely not a WMU fan and also likely not a fan of me previously, but he *was* a fan of Justin and our team culture. Going from rivals to friends shows the power of that culture and illustrates what Row the Boat can do to connect people. We all became close and will continue to stay close because of our mission together through football, serving, and giving.

One of my favorite things about Row the Boat is to see all the people it has impacted in education, healthcare, and the military. People like Cody Pulju, a middle school teacher in Minnesota who utilizes the Row the Boat principles to impact more students. And John Foss, the VP of Hospital Operations at Mercy Health, who said that he used Row the Boat to reignite and rebuild his team and had their best year in over a decade as a result. I've heard from nurses who have used Row the Boat to energize their departments and principals who inspired and equipped their teachers and students with it. And as someone who studies military history, I also love hearing from leaders in our armed forces who have been inspired by and have utilized Row the Boat to motivate their people. As I said in the beginning of the book, my goal in creating Row the Boat was not just to win football games but to help people win in life. I'm thankful we are able to live and share this mission each day.

Chapter 13

Rowing into the Future

Jon Gordon

Row the Boat

While books have a beginning and an end, the Row the Boat journey continues. As you read these words, the next chapter of Row the Boat will have already been written, not on a page, but in the book of life. More seasons will be played, more players will be encouraged, more people will be impacted, and more stories will be told. Fittingly, I'm writing this on December 31, 2020, a day to reflect on what has happened in the past and think about the future you want to create. With all that P.J. and Row the Boat have accomplished, I asked him what's next. What does he see for the future? Where does Row the Boat go from here? P.J.'s answers are a great way to finish this book as he begins the next part of his Row the Boat journey.

Rowing into the Future

Chapter 14

Where Do You Row the Boat from Here?

P.J. Fleck

108

Row the Boat

Make Today Better—Change Your Best

So where do we go from here? How does Row the Boat continue on the journey? I return to advice that taught me so much about football, business, and life from one of my greatest mentors, Jim Tressel.

"Don't *ever* think you're the only one who can do what you're doing at the place you're doing it at. We all have an expiration date. Leave it better than you found it. Nothing is guaranteed in college football or life. Be more than just football and wins." Wow! Basically, he told me that people are everything in this world and you make success happen *together*. Always understand that you're an influencer for only a short period in history. What will you be remembered for? What will be your legacy? Is it the wins, how you made people feel, the lives you changed, the moments and memories you created for others, or the hope you instilled in people— or maybe all of it? Of course, I love to win. I am as competitive as they come, and I'm a football coach. But truth be told, what Heather and I love most about Rowing the Boat is making a difference in people's lives, and coaching gives us a platform to do that in a lot of ways with a lot of people. How will you use your platform for purposeful change? I love to encourage people and give them hope. I love to help people focus on the possibility of what can be done instead of so many focusing on what they cannot do.

Be the Reason

Adversity has taught me that we *can* overcome anything. We *can* find a way forward and we *can* row out of any storm.

Thinking back to 2020, it was not the year to get all we wanted, but to be grateful for what we had. The price of change is expensive and not everything will be perfect, but we can make each other better and we can help others see possibilities instead of impossibilities. Football teams, families, and businesses are not always going to have the most resources, the greatest skill, the most money, the biggest brand, the most demand, the most support, the cleanest bill of health, the perfect family dynamics, and/or the best facilities. However, it's important to remember that if you don't have it, you can create it! Row the Boat each day and create the change you want to see. When you hit adversity, keep rowing. If you face a storm, keep rowing. When the winds are against you, keep rowing. There will always be a lot of reasons why you can't do something. Find a way to be the reason why you can!

Keep Rowing

We're going to keep rowing one day at a time and keep impacting lives. If you look too far into future, you'll lose your focus and energy in the present. So right *now* we are going to continue to live and share the principles of Row the Boat with others. We are going to continue to live the standards we have set for ourselves and our culture. Heather is expanding her role with organizations to partner up to spread the Row the Boat mission. She's working with companies like Ronald McDonald House and the apparel companies UNRL, Love Your Melon, and Chubbies, to expand our outreach.

I'm going to continue to improve. I won't compare my journey or my boat to others. That will steal my joy. Instead,

I will focus on my own Row the Boat journey while helping others create their own boats and enjoy their own journeys. When you do, life becomes a special ride. It becomes more about your significance, influence, and legacy rather than just your success. I'm so fortunate to already be living my dream; my goal is to now empower others to live theirs!

I want to share 10 lessons I've learned that will continue to guide me forward. I hope they inspire you.

1. Never sacrifice what you really want down the road for what you want right now.

2. Trained behavior creates boring habits; boring habits create elite instincts.

3. You win with *people,* not just players—people who make their life about others.

4. Do all you can to give more than you take because serving and giving is the key to life.

5. The hardest part about being the standard is that *you* are the standard *all* the time.

6. Culture trumps skill.

7. A person distracted is a person defeated.

8. Embrace your past to create your future.

9. Hard work and competitive spirit are *not* the same. Always compete!

10. There is a major difference between success and significance. The goal should be significance. Row Your Boat!

Other Resources

For more information about the Row the Boat principles and/or to support the *Fleck Family Fund* at the University of Minnesota's Masonic Children's Hospital, please visit our website at RowtheBoat.org.

Other Books by Jon Gordon

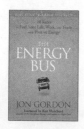

The Energy Bus

A man whose life and career are in shambles learns from a unique bus driver and set of passengers how to overcome adversity. Enjoy an enlightening ride of positive energy that is improving the way leaders lead, employees work, and teams function.

www.TheEnergyBus.com

The No Complaining Rule

Follow a VP of Human Resources who must save herself and her company from ruin and discover proven principles and an actionable plan to win the battle against individual and organizational negativity.

www.NoComplainingRule.com

Training Camp

This inspirational story about a small guy with a big heart, and a special coach who guides him on a quest for excellence, reveals the 11 winning habits that separate the best individuals and teams from the rest.

www.TrainingCamp11.com

The Shark and the Goldfish

Delightfully illustrated, this quick read is packed with tips and strategies on how to respond to challenges beyond your control in order to thrive during waves of change.

www.SharkandGoldfish.com

Soup

The newly appointed CEO of a popular soup company is brought in to reinvigorate the brand and bring success back to a company that has fallen on hard times. Through her journey, discover the key ingredients to unite, engage, and inspire teams to create a culture of greatness.

www.Soup11.com

The Seed

Go on a quest for the meaning and passion behind work with Josh, an up-and-comer at his company who is disenchanted with his job. Through Josh's cross-country journey, you'll find surprising new sources of wisdom and inspiration in your own business and life.

www.Seed11.com

One Word

One Word is a simple concept that delivers powerful life change! This quick read will inspire you to simplify your life and work by focusing on just one word for this year. *One Word* creates clarity, power, passion, and life-change. When you find your word, live it, and share it, your life will become more rewarding and exciting than ever.

www.getoneword.com

The Positive Dog

We all have two dogs inside of us. One dog is positive, happy, optimistic, and hopeful. The other dog is negative, mad, pessimistic, and fearful. These two dogs often fight inside us, but guess who wins? The one you feed the most. *The Positive Dog* is an inspiring story that not only reveals the strategies and benefits of being positive, but also an essential truth: being positive doesn't just make you better; it makes everyone around you better.

www.feedthepositivedog.com

Other Books by Jon Gordon

The Carpenter

The Carpenter is Jon Gordon's most inspiring book yet—filled with powerful lessons and success strategies. Michael wakes up in the hospital with a bandage on his head and fear in his heart after collapsing during a morning jog. When Michael finds out the man who saved his life is a carpenter, he visits him and quickly learns that he is more than just a carpenter; he is also a builder of lives, careers, people, and teams. In this journey, you will learn timeless principles to help you stand out, excel, and make an impact on people and the world.

www.carpenter11.com

The Hard Hat

A true story about Cornell lacrosse player George Boiardi, *The Hard Hat* is an unforgettable book about a selfless, loyal, joyful, hard-working, competitive, and compassionate leader and teammate, the impact he had on his team and program, and the lessons we can learn from him. This inspirational story will teach you how to build a great team and be the best teammate you can be.

www.hardhat21.com

You Win in the Locker Room First

Based on the extraordinary experiences of NFL Coach Mike Smith and leadership expert Jon Gordon, *You Win in the Locker Room First* offers a rare, behind-the-scenes look at one of the most pressure-packed leadership jobs on the planet, and what leaders can learn from these experiences in order to build their own winning teams.

www.wininthelockerroom.com

Life Word

Life Word reveals a simple, powerful tool to help you identify the word that will inspire you to live your best life while leaving your greatest legacy. In the process, you'll discover your why, which will help show you how to live with a renewed sense of power, purpose, and passion.

www.getoneword.com/lifeword

The Power of Positive Leadership

The Power of Positive Leadership is your personal coach for becoming the leader your people deserve. Jon Gordon gathers insights from his bestselling fables to bring you the definitive guide to positive leadership. Difficult times call for leaders who are up to the challenge. Results are the by product of your culture, teamwork, vision, talent, innovation, execution, and commitment. This book shows you how to bring it all together to become a powerfully positive leader.

www.powerofpositiveleadership.com

The Power of a Positive Team

In *The Power of a Positive Team*, Jon Gordon draws on his unique team-building experience, as well as conversations with some of the greatest teams in history, to provide an essential framework of proven practices to empower teams to work together more effectively and achieve superior results.

www.PowerOfAPositiveTeam.com

The Coffee Bean

From bestselling author Jon Gordon and rising star Damon West comes *The Coffee Bean*: an illustrated fable that teaches readers how to transform their environment, overcome challenges, and create positive change.

www.coffeebeanbook.com

Stay Positive

Fuel yourself and others with positive energy—inspirational quotes and encouraging messages to live by from bestselling author, Jon Gordon. Keep this little book by your side, read from it each day, and feed your mind, body, and soul with the power of positivity.

www.StayPositiveBook.com

The Garden

The Garden is an enlightening and encouraging fable that helps readers overcome The 5 D's (doubt, distortion, discouragement, distractions, and division) in order to find more peace, focus, connection, and happiness. Jon tells a story of teenage twins who, through the help of a neighbor and his special garden, find ancient wisdom, life-changing lessons, and practical strategies to overcome the fear, anxiety, and stress in their lives.

www.readthegarden.com

Relationship Grit

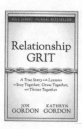

Bestselling author Jon Gordon is back with another life-affirming book. This time, he teams up with Kathryn Gordon, his wife of 23 years, for a look at what it takes to build strong relationships. In *Relationship Grit*, the Gordons reveal what brought them together, what kept them together through difficult times, and what continues to sustain their love and passion for one another to this day.

www.relationshipgritbook.com

Stick Together

From bestselling author Jon Gordon and coauthor Kate Leavell, *Stick Together* delivers a crucial message about the power of belief, ownership, connection, love, inclusion, consistency, and hope. The authors guide individuals and teams on an inspiring journey to show them how to persevere through challenges, overcome obstacles, and create success together.

www.sticktogetherbook.com

The Energy Bus for Kids

The illustrated children's adaptation of the bestselling book *The Energy Bus* tells the story of George, who, with the help of his school bus driver, Joy, learns that if he believes in himself, he'll find the strength to overcome any challenge. His journey teaches kids how to overcome negativity, bullies, and everyday challenges to be their best.

www.EnergyBusKids.com

Thank You and Good Night

Thank You and Good Night is a beautifully illustrated book that shares the heart of gratitude. Jon Gordon takes a little boy and girl on a fun-filled journey from one perfect moonlit night to the next. During their adventurous days and nights, the children explore the people, places, and things they are thankful for.

The Hard Hat for Kids

The Hard Hat for Kids is an illustrated guide to teamwork. Adapted from the bestseller *The Hard Hat*, this uplifting story presents practical insights and life-changing lessons that are immediately applicable to everyday situations, giving kids—and adults—a new outlook on cooperation, friendship, and the selfless nature of true teamwork.

www.HardHatforKids.com

One Word for Kids

If you could choose only one word to help you have your best year ever, what would it be? *Love? Fun? Believe? Brave?* It's probably different for each person. How you find your word is just as important as the word itself. And once you know your word, what do you do with it? In *One Word for Kids,* bestselling author Jon Gordon—along with coauthors Dan Britton and Jimmy Page—asks these questions to children and adults of all ages, teaching an important life lesson in the process.

www.getoneword.com/kids

Other Books by Jon Gordon

The Coffee Bean for Kids

From the bestselling authors of *The Coffee Bean*, inspire and encourage children with this transformative tale of personal strength. Perfect for parents, teachers, and children who wish to overcome negativity and challenging situations, *The Coffee Bean for Kids* teaches readers about the potential that each one of us has to lead, influence, and make a positive impact on others and the world.

www.coffeebeankidsbook.com